Monkeys
Making a Difference

by Reggie Winbush

Harcourt
SCHOOL PUBLISHERS

Cover, p.4, p.13, ©Melanie Stetson Freeman/The Christian Science Monitor via Getty Images; p.3, ©AP Photo/Leslie Mazoch; p.5, ©Najlah Feanny/CORBIS SABA; p.6, ©Jeffrey L. Rotman/CORBIS; p.7, ©BananaStock/PunchStock; p.8, ©The Sacramento Bee/Dick Schmidt/ZUMA Press; p.9, ©AP Photo/The Daily Reporter, Karen Lee Mikols; p.10, p.11, p.12, p.14, ©JIM BOURG/Reuters/Corbis.

Printed in China

ISBN 10: 0-15-350670-9
ISBN 13: 978-0-15-350670-3

Ordering Options
ISBN 10: 0-15-350600-8 (Grade 3 On-Level Collection)
ISBN 13: 978-0-15-350600-0 (Grade 3 On-Level Collection)
ISBN 10: 0-15-357885-8 (package of 5)
ISBN 13: 978-0-15-357885-4 (package of 5)

5 6 7 8 9 10 985 12 11 10 09

Trina's Helper

Trina finds the book she wants to read. She does not pick it up, though. "Sam, fetch," she says, calmly.

Trina holds a pointer in her mouth. She points it at the book, and a tiny red dot appears. Then she points it at a stand, and now the red dot is there. Sam gets the book, puts it on the stand, and flips it open.

"Good boy, Sam!" says Trina.

Sam is not a robot. He is not a dog. Sam is a monkey.

Trina uses a wheelchair because she can't move her arms or her legs. Monkeys like Sam make Trina's life easier.

Monkeys make good helpers because they have hands. They can pick things up, they can open bottles, and they can turn doorknobs.

However, not just any monkey will do. Sam is a capuchin monkey. Capuchin monkeys weigh less than ten pounds (4.5 kg), and they are about eighteen inches (45.7 cm) tall. They can sit on a person's shoulder, and they can fit into small places.

Helping Hands

Dr. Mary Joan Willard had the idea for monkey helpers and formed Helping Hands in 1977. Helping Hands trains the monkeys, finds people who need help, and teaches them how to work together.

At first, Dr. Willard used adult monkey helpers, but young monkeys are easier to train because they learn to obey at an early age. Helping Hands monkeys are born at a nearby zoo.

Part of the Family

Monkey helpers need to get used to living with people, so they move in with foster families when they are about two months old. The families raise the monkeys for about four years.

At first, family members feed the monkeys with bottles. Then the monkeys grow teeth. They can eat special monkey food. They have treats, too. Oranges and grapes are some of their favorites. This might be because of their wonderful scent.

The monkeys live in large cages, which are put in busy areas. That way, the monkeys are always around people. Of course, the monkeys are not always in their cages. They need time outside of their cages to exercise.

The monkeys are like little children. They are very active, and they like to play. Cuddling and holding is important because that helps the monkeys feel good.

Monkey helpers will go many different places. Family members can prepare them for this.

The monkeys learn to ride in cars, and they patrol stores with their families to meet other people. This is very easy because people are curious. They approach the monkeys, and they ask about them. The monkeys learn to be calm and friendly.

Families grow to love their monkeys, and the monkeys love them, too. However, the monkeys must leave. They need to do more to get ready to become helpers. It is time for them to go to Monkey College.

Monkey College

The monkeys return to Helping Hands where they meet their trainers. The trainers get to know their monkeys, and they see how each monkey learns. One monkey may learn words quickly. Another may learn from watching.

Some monkeys may need more time, so the trainers slow down. Some monkeys may need to take breaks, although no monkey helper has ever whined about the hard work! They may just need time to be silly. The trainers let them relax, and then it's time to work again.

Capuchin monkeys make good students. They are very clever. They solve problems, and they also copy people's actions.

Training takes time, and each skill is broken into small steps. The trainer will demonstrate each step. The trainer speaks while she acts, and she uses the monkey's name in the command.

The monkey watches, and then the monkey tries. It gets it right! "Good job!" exclaims the trainer, and then she gives the monkey a treat.

The monkey learns about the pointer next.
The pointer shines a dot of light on what the
person wants. The monkey must get it.

The trainer points the light at a can. The
monkey looks. Then it wanders over to the
table and brings back a book. It is not right,
so there is no treat, and it must try again.
The monkey looks, it sees the red dot, and it
brings the can. The monkey gets the treat, and
soon it understands the link between the dot
and the command.

Teaming Up

Monkey College can take one to two years. No monkeys fail because all learn in time.

The people at Helping Hands think about each monkey when placing it with an owner. Some monkeys are calm, so they go with quiet people. Some are very active, so they are matched with busy people.

The new owners prepare. They get what they need for the monkeys. Some may even get a machine for their wheelchair that gives out monkey treats.

Then it is time to go home. A trainer goes with the monkey. The trainer stays for about a week to help the monkey and its new owner work together.

The owner practices with the pointer, he learns commands, and he finds out what the monkey can do. After a week, the trainer leaves. Then they are on their own.

What do the monkeys do? They fetch things, and they get drinks. They even put straws in them. They put CDs or DVDs into a computer. They scratch itches, and they comb hair.

These may seem like little things, but they make a big difference. The monkeys make people more independent.

Computers can obey voice commands, and machines can pick things up. However, monkeys can listen, they can give hugs, and monkeys can certainly make someone laugh.

The monkeys can live more than twenty years. They are lifetime helpers, and they are also lifetime friends.

More people are learning about these monkeys and want them. It is easy to see why. These special little monkeys change lives.

Think Critically

1. Why are capuchin monkeys good helpers?

2. The story says that monkeys love their foster families. Is that a fact or an opinion?

3. Why do people want to approach the monkeys in public?

4. How do the monkeys make people feel independent?

5. Would it bother you for someone to bring a monkey into a place like a store or school? Why or why not?

 Social Studies

Look It Up Look up capuchin monkeys in an encyclopedia or on the Internet. List three countries where they live in the wild. Find the countries on a map.

School-Home Connection Capuchin monkeys weigh less than ten pounds (4.5 kg). They are about eighteen inches (45.7 cm) tall. Find objects of this size in your home.